# This is for MEN!

*By Curtis J Hines*

*Copyright © 2021*

*by Curtis J Hines*

# Table of Content

*Disclaimer*

*About the Author*

*Purpose*

*Let's be clear*

*The Question*

*Mind/Behaviors*

*Body/Health*

*Sex*

*Mission/Goals/Dreams*

*Finances/Money*

*Legacy/Footprints*

*You do MATTER!*

*"Imagine that? Another man pretending to be you, giving your significant other what she deserves and raising your kids... Is that what you want? NO!? So, Stop heading that way! There's no one better than you! No one can do it like YOU!"*

**-Curtis J Hines**

*Man – Husband - Father - King*

# Disclaimer

In no means do I profess to being a doctor or a therapist nor do I have any degrees or certifications in psychology or an expert on behavior. The words in this book are of my own from my personal experience as a father, husband and man. I do not guarantee that any of what you read will fix any situation you're in. I write this as a testimony of the life I've lived so far. I hope that what you read in this book will enlighten you in the many challenging areas you have as man, father and/or husband. I hope that it gives you a more positive and practical perspective when seeking ways to adjust with committing to your commitments.

## About the Author

Curtis J. Hines was born and raised in the inner city of Memphis, TN. Graduate of Booker T. Washington High School (Memphis), studied at Orange Coast College, (Costa Mesa, CA), father of five amazing kids and husband to his soul mate, Lashanda. He is a God-fearing man! He also has three published books, "Which Way to Go", "Which Way to Go Now" and "Sex Credit". He's a Motivational Speaker, with a 52-week inspirational journal and video series on YouTube called, "Committing to Your Commitments.

For more about him check out his social media pages @thecurtisjhines on Facebook, Instagram, TikTok and Twitter.

## Purpose

To inspire and motivate all men from every corner of the world to be faithful to himself, his children, his community and to the commitment he made with his wife. To help men understand the many challenges and temptations of life, to be aware of the consequences of one's choices and how they affect not only himself, but those he's committed to as well. Educate men on building a financial foundation to support himself and his family. To give knowledge that leads to making better decisions to living a healthier life and aware of health risks.

## Let's be clear:

**Man:** *an adult male- the opposite of woman*

**Husband:** *a married man, especially when considered in relation to his partner in marriage- the opposite of wife*

**Father:** *a male parent- the opposite of mother*

**King:** *a male sovereign, monarch; a man who holds by life tenure, and usually by hereditary right, the chief authority over a country and people. The male crown holder! -the opposite of Queen*

Now that we've defined the terms, let's be clear about what it takes to walk in those shoes. Age is just a number. Let me repeat that… AGE IS JUST A NUMBER! Yes, by law when you're 18 in some places and by 21 in others, you're considered a grown up, an adult. Yes, getting some one pregnant then she delivers that baby, it in fact makes you a dad. Yes, if you sign official documents and say, "I do", you are legally someone's husband. Finally, a long time ago you could be up next to inherit the rights to be a king.

Okay, now that we got that out the way for the smart asses, let's get deeper than the general meaning of those "WORDS". Age has nothing to do with you fulfilling these roles as you should. Many pretend but that will only get you so far. It takes guts, and a whole lot of patience to truly live up to being a great father, man, husband and having a King's state of mind.

Through this book I will talk about what it takes to be a better man overall from my personal experience through the thirty-eight years I lived so far. "I'm a grown man!" The 21-year-old me would shout when I felt someone was trying to tell me how to live my life at that time. In hindsight, they were giving me great advice. I honestly had no clue what it truly meant at the age. But now, I'm a professional adult. Funny, I know. Everyone is a professional at something right? I'm well-seasoned I must say. I claim that title based on my actions and commitment to my commitments. I have been a father for over twenty years now with a total of five kids, a husband for over fifteen years and counting. I believe I have a King's mentality now, which has been activated for over the last six years.

    I say the last six years because I wasn't being true to my commitments during a few of the earlier years as a father and a husband. I wasn't giving it my all. I had challenges with giving the necessary time and attention in those areas I needed to focus on the most. Through trials and tribulations, on top of a lot of picking my ass up off the ground, I have managed to figure it all out for the most part.

We all have our own definition of success. I sincerely mean every word I wrote in this book through my perspective and what I've lived through so far. I do not take any of this lightly nor do I want anyone else to. This serves as a reminder to myself on how far I've come. I share this information with you in hopes it triggers something within you to move you towards a better way of living as a man, father and husband. I'm going to say this, which you may hear a few times as you continue to read…

**TAKE IT ONE DAY AT A TIME!**

**What are you doing today to become better?**

That is the ultimate question you must ask yourself daily to challenge yourself in all the areas you seek to improve.

Let's start with the most significant piece of the puzzle to making major adjustments in your life.

# Mind/Behaviors

**To live up to your own expectations and becoming the man you truly desire to be, it starts in the mind.**

The mind is the key to unlocking the lifestyle you need to be better. It's a lifestyle change. You are the head. You are the head of the family, the head of the house and the head when it comes to some of the most important responsibilities to keep the family together and balanced. You're either causing an avalanche of chaos that destroys or creating a waterfall that provides water which helps with the growth of your seeds, family, relationships and friendships. How you think and act is highly contagious. Your ability to break or build yourself and your family just from the perspectives you have on everything shouldn't be taken for granted.

Just like the word says, "As a man thinketh in his heart so shall he be…" Please understand how crucial it is that you are careful about what you're feeding your mind. Whatever negative desires or wrong turns are made; it always resonates in the mind first. It's never split decisions either. They are decisions that have been marinating in your daily thoughts.

Investing your time and giving attention towards things that are useless to your wellbeing is toxic. You're sacrificing too much. You can't be positive if you don't think positive thoughts. It is IMPOSSIBLE! Let me know when you master that then contact me as soon as possible. I haven't seen or heard of anyone doing it. It's a fight, you'll lose every time. I'm like 0-50 when it comes to generating meaningful outcomes while digesting negativity.

There is an upside. Another side of the coin. It works the same way with positive outcomes and better choices. The more you download positivity, significant ideas and thoughts (which is what is best for you, your family and lifestyle), you will produce that.

Remember, what's in the mind flows outward with actions. Some days will be better than others. I have yet to have a perfect day, week or month. BUT... The more you make it a priority to manifest healthier thinking the easier it becomes to control what you put in your mental database. You will have the upper hand when filtering what passes through your mind. There's no refresh button or reset button to clear your head of what's in there already. Oh, how we wish we could forget some encounters, friendships or that one-night sta…. You know what I'm saying! I have discovered that if you can minimize the old way of thinking you overload on better perspectives on life. One step in the direction is giving yourself permission to move on from the old you.

**Release it!** Letting go of past hurt, habits and pain is essential to helping yourself become better at what's steering your behaviors into a satisfying future. As men, we tend to ignore a lot of the reasons we react the way we do as we get older, it's because of past experiences dealing with torn and uncomfortable emotions.

We find it hard to admit it yet alone to address it. In order to move forward, you must let go of the issues that are holding you back from adjusting. If you refuse to release them, you'll continue to pull that dead weight into every relationship, friendship and even passing it down to your kids. Battling those never-ending thoughts of your mom, dad, or any family or friends that's wronged you without you ever having a voice or the courage to rectify the pain they caused. This will have you taking it out on any and every one that triggers you in any way close to that prior trauma. I understand that some things are harder than others to push through. To just stop worrying about it or forget about it. Believe me, I get it and totally understand.

Some people do react differently while carrying the burdens of childhood trauma. Again, this is the biggest turning point of your life that will push you forward into that better man, father and husband you desire to be. It will always be difficult for anyone to get through to you when they're being punished for pain they didn't cause or do to you.

I've seen it happen many times to my friends and family from someone else, and I've also done it myself. I leaned on the fact that my dad wasn't a part of my life and not having the best relationship with my mom and sisters to make me feel better about not doing my best when came to my responsibilities.

I filled my head with excuses that led me to treat others like crap, knowing they deserved better from me. I wasn't in control of my thoughts. I didn't let go of those past frustrations I felt that my dad left with me when he abandoned me to go live his own life. It was more of a fear I had than anything else once I finally became a father myself. It was the fear of not living up to being a great father. It was fear of not being there for my kids. I was afraid I was going to be just like him.

For the record, I don't think my pops was a bad person for not being in my life. I understand it now. It was just his way of thinking that caused him not to be there. Something he believed, something he put in his mind caused him not to be there, whatever that was. So, yeah, I wouldn't allow myself to get too attached to anyone. When I felt things were going great, I got scared knowing that it was a matter of time I was going to screw it all up somehow.

For years I plagued my mind with those kinds of thoughts. It crippled me for too long, always afraid that I was going to end up walking away from the relationships and people that needed me the most. It was all in my head. I had to shake out of that to move forward. It was impossible for me to continue to live that way if I wanted to become a better man not only for myself but for everyone who deserve the best version of me.

As men we poison ourselves thinking we have everything under control while avoiding the deeper, darker chaos within ourselves that holds us captive as prisoners. You must break free. You must change that! You have to find beneficial approaches to release that hurt. Trust me, and it is not drugs or alcohol! Those will not help at all!

**Check Yourself!** Being a spiritual man myself, I had to do some serious soul searching. I was secretly blaming everyone for being the reasons why I wasn't as successful as I thought I should be. I was pointing the finger at everyone but myself on why my life wasn't in order. I was looking at everyone else but the man in the mirror. It was easy doing that for years. The more people I friended, my family members that stuck around doing my worse days, I found a way to believe they were my problems. They were the ones holding me back. They were the ones not pushing me to be great or keeping me from doing whatever it was I thought I wanted to do at the time. The excuses were piling up every day, week after week, year after the year. Until you run everyone off.

Once you've run off everyone you blamed for your failures, that's when it hurts the most. Maybe you haven't made it that far in the blame game which is great. Trust me... Don't! If you can tap out now, please do. But if you have, then you know that feeling. It's not a pleasant one at all. That's when you know it's time to tighten up. There's no one else to blame. You've ran out of people to point at. It's time to turn it all around. Here are the steps I took to rearrange my thinking.

**Do something about it!** Praying was first for me. I had to reconnect with what I knew on a spiritual level. I grew up in the church. I had a relationship with God that I somehow strayed away from. I was ignoring everything I knew about having faith and hope that things were always going to work out regardless of the troubles I was getting myself into when it came to how I was thinking. I didn't lean on God at all when I continued to hold on to the hurt others cause from my childhood. I knew better than that, but it was much easier to not forgive or forget. But hey, if you're not into religious living, I get it. No pressure from me... But, for me, it helped!

Another way to pick yourself after the dust settles and you're all alone. It was uneasy at first, yet it gave me so much hope. A blessing in disguise. I made serious efforts positioning myself around positive males. I had to seek other men I knew that were opened enough to share their life lessons with me. There's always someone right there in your face ready to reveal how their life got turned upside down due to negative thinking. It will sound the same as what you're going through. Like how holding on to past grudges or pain is pointless and exhausting. Usually from someone that's lived a little. Someone that can give you some serious advice that will help you understand that you're not alone.

It's usually that seasoned coworker that's always trying to tell you about how it used to be when he was doing this or that, the guy at the gym that makes comments about uplifting things he's doing or even the older gentlemen at the church that speaks to you and your family all the time. There are people that's ready to help you if only you would speak up. Set the pride aside that's been pulling you away from the help you need.

Stop kidding yourself. Men thinking, we know it all, and then having the audacity to believe it's just you that's dealing with challenges from your past. The more you can vent to those that have experienced similar events or that's familiar with carrying past weight, the easy it will be for you to slowly let it go. You'll realize that so many people have been in your shoes when it comes to let downs by the people that should have been there for you when you were growing up. You'll stop being ashamed of your past. You'll finally understand why you react the way you do to committing to relationships, trusting and being completely honest with people.

There will be a huge release you will feel once you start to become fully aware of yourself. Once you clean out toxic stuff you've been holding on to in your head, you will then have room to put in new information. Creating better memories. You can now work on controlling what you think about. Focus on what's being placed on your mind. Your thoughts... Let's continue with more approaches that have helped me.

**Positive routines... Controlling what you put in your mind.** Every morning I wake up, I say "Thank you!" I start my day with gratitude. It automatically puts me in a great mood and gives me a feeling of being grateful. I don't think about anything from the night before that wasn't handled or thought out before I went to bed. My focus is what positive factors I'm going to accomplish that day. I mentally or physically make a list in my head or on paper about what needs to get done that day. If I can physically do it, it's going to get done. I plan it all out then I pray about the plan I've made. I ask God for the courage, strength and path to take to ensure I complete the list. If it's his will, let be done.

**Meditating** is a must. I personally believe in it. It's part of my morning ritual. I make time to meditate on seeing those tasks from my list already done. I see myself executing my ideas, daily goals and checking off items on my to do list. I vision the bigger picture. I hold on to the feeling of completion. I watch or listen to motivational, inspirational videos or podcasts to continue that positive thinking throughout my day. I even have to shy away from trap music I use to listen to early in the mornings thinking it was getting me hyped to start my day. That music was just waking my sleepy self-up... That's it. It wasn't the best way to prepare to write this book or going into my job, after listening to someone talk about robbing and getting money by shooting at your haters if they disrespect you. Hey, if it helps you without causing any disruptions to how you react to people or your work, then more power to you. For me... I wasn't giving myself the best food for my thoughts.

    You must constantly consciencely program your thoughts. You are downloading and planting the seeds of motivation you need. You are programming the mind you want to have when going out into the world as well as when you're working on controlling your mind. The slightest negative interaction, comment or news can disturb your peace. You must build resilience when it comes to keeping that positive mindset throughout your day-to-day life. I've learned that you must be careful when interacting with people you determine are on a negative frequency. Far too many times we allow people's toxic energy to infiltrate our good mood.

Can you recall the times you were feeling great that morning or day and as soon as you talked to someone that was in a bad mood it immediately killed your great vibes or peace? Especially at the end of a stress-free day. It attaches itself on to you and causes you to go to sleep with weight that's not yours to carry. Or the entire day is heavy because of someone else negative vibes have been laid on your shoulders. You are responsible for protecting your peace of mind and how you respond to any negativity from others. That's why it's so important to work on what you put in your head. Enough good thoughts will always outweigh a few negative ones. Once you've gained that kind of control over what's in your head, you'll be able to give out those actions as well. It effects your behavior in a wonderful way. You will care more about the situations and people that matter the most. Not only will you be giving yourself the best you, but you'll be also giving those around you the same thing. There's no way to treat yourself like crap if you're feeding yourself positivity daily. No way you're going to treat those around you like they don't matter if you're feeding yourself positive thoughts every day. You will have very encouraging habits that will benefit everyone that's in your life. It will show in what you do. You don't have to make people believe what you say if you're showing them what's on your mind. Your actions will reflect the actions of someone who loves himself and others.

Also, Day to day routines help build consistency. It starts with giving a damn about what and how you're representing yourself as well as the people you're responsible for. If you read one hour a day, you're going to maximize your vocabulary and knowledge compared to someone who only reads once every six months. Ever heard of the saying, "It's what we don't know, that kills us..." Flood your mind with information. It's worth the time and energy to educate yourself. We have so many distractions forcing us to pay attention to useless things. How much time do you spend on social media? How much time do you spend arguing about sports? How much time you spend binge watching some TV series? Hours that you can't get back! Can you afford that right now? Think about what you can learn or what you could get done with that same time. Don't get me wrong, there's nothing wrong with any of that. If you're blowing through your daily tasks, getting things done without any issues or lag. You earned the right to scroll a little and watch some TV. That's the only time I'm on social media or watching any TV personally. I had to earn it. If I spend most of my day scrolling Facebook or Instagram without checking off items on my daily list, then I've failed not only myself but my family and other responsibilities. There are some benefits being on social media which I'll get into later. Your day-to-day routine is all about polishing your behaviors to learn more than what you knew the day before. To spend as much time as you can on what's helping you overall instead of watching everyone else live their dreams. One day at a time. It takes patience. Please believe it's worth it because you're worth it!

**It's contagious!** Once you have programmed your mind to focus on what's important in your world when it comes to going after your goals and dreams, it will allow you to spread that energy around. Your dedication to better yourself will flow into your family and friends naturally. It will impact the way you treat others. When your wife or girlfriend see the work you're putting in to becoming a better you, imagine what that's going to do for them. Think about how that's going to influence them. Your kids will see it as well. That's who's watching you the most. As a father it is a wonderful thing to have your kids looking up to you as their role model because you're displaying what they need to reciprocate. Not only will they see it, but they'll also feel it! So, imagine SHOWING your spouse and your kids you love them every day because that's what you're proving to yourself. Having control of your thoughts, your behaviors in a positive way is self-love. That's the self-focus you need. Loving yourself enough to make the correct changes to be the best version of yourself.

When you are executing your daily routine, it opens you up to be more helpful. One thing I noticed when I was adjusting to being highly productive every day, I wanted everyone around me to be too. "If I can do it, they can too", was something I started to feel when I was witnessing my wife and kids struggling to focus or complete the things they needed to get done. I was able to notice their areas of opportunities that required motivation and a change of behavior. That too became part of my daddy/husband duties.

Imagine ironing your wife's clothes every day for her because you know she hates to iron. Imagine studying with your kids daily because they can't seem to remember to do that especially important thing. You know kids, "Oh I forgot!" Instead of discipling them, I started to work with them. Imagine cooking your family's favorite meal to give your wife a break in the kitchen. Imagine researching the tools your wife or kids need to help them chase those ideas they have put on hold because they weren't as disciplined as you to just do it. Most people if given just a slight push, would get the ball rolling with a goal or dream they had or have. Imagine being the one pushing your wife and kids to accomplish something they had doubts about. You can! If you're in control of your thoughts and behaviors, it is very possible for you, just as it is for the rest of your family!

**Change can happen instantly!** They say it takes 21 days to change a bad habit or to shift your life in any direction. I believe that is true. I also believe it can take only one day. I believe once you reach a certain point mentally in your life, rather it be from frustrations or hitting rock bottom to having a vision or a dream flash before your eyes. You can instantly generate enough will power to make you alter your entire life. I say that because I experienced that myself. It didn't take 21 days for me to stop drinking. It took me waking up in ICU with my wife and mother standing over me in tears to realize drinking wasn't going to control my life anymore. Having a doctor tell you that they almost lost you should scare you enough to make you change your way of living immediately. From that day forward, I never thought about alcohol again. Not even for a second. I was done! It may take something like that for some to change but I hope that it doesn't take you to hit a hard place in your life before you decide to take control of your thoughts and behaviors. If you continue doing something that helps the people you love, those are great behaviors to have. Who's going to complain about that? No more headaches from those people fussing about why you're not doing this or not doing that. That focus brings peace and happiness everyone can enjoy. It starts with you. It's tough but it's worth it!

**Talk to me Doc!** Therapy is key too. From conversations with many men through the years, there's a sense of pride that keeps us from seeking professional help. I'm still not sure why or when we made it an embarrassing decision to get professional help in the area of mental health. I admit I was guilty of looking at it that way myself, after sharing more personal information with certain people I admired. I was assuming they had their lives completely together, until they revealed that they were speaking with a therapist on a regular basis! That alone eliminated all of my excuses. It made it easier for me to take that next step. With that being said, I have seen a therapist in my past which was a great help for me overcoming a lot of self-doubt and forgiving myself for all the self-sabotaging I did over the years. So, fellas, PLEASE don't allow anyone or anything keep you from seeking that kind of support. Especially if you're at the edge with thoughts of giving up! PLEASE, if you're deciding if your life isn't worth living due to the many mistakes you've made, or you feel you can't do anything right, GET HELP NOW! That's a lie! You can get things back on track! There are so many websites and numbers you can go on or call to get the help you need from a professional. I HOPE AND PRAY THAT YOU TAKE YOURSELF SERIOUS ENOUGH TO WANT TO KEEP FIGHTING! PLEASE DON'T GIVE UP!

**Understand this...** It will take some time for everyone to adjust with your new way of thinking and living if your norm has always been rocky. Like I mentioned before, I was an alcoholic. As crazy as it sounds, everyone wasn't all celebrating the transitions right away. I had to do some major work on myself to get those around me on board. It may be a different story I hope for you. I say that because again, you can't let others be your excuse for not working twice as hard towards a better you. It was easy to blame them for not encouraging me to continue the new outlook I had on life since I gave up drinking. Thinking they had to change just as quick as I did wasn't fair for them. One thing it showed me was who my real friends were verses who were the triggers to my addictions. There were two types of people I associated with back then. Ones that were all about the fun, drinking and partying side of me. The others were heartbroken because of my lack of stability. My life was spiraling out of control from being out all day and night drinking until early morning, struggling to maintain a job and destroying my body from within. The choice became clear with who I owed for loving and caring about me. Once the drinking stopped, the people that didn't like the "stay at home and work on yourself, family, health and future Curtis", stopped calling, texting and offering to come by yet alone invited me to do anything with them. It only took a few weeks, maybe a month for that to sit in. I realized how those people never meant any good for my life. It wasn't until then when the smoke cleared who had always been there for me. I had to prove it to myself first that I was all in on the new lifestyle. The behaviors they had to endure during my challenging years with my past, mixed with an alcohol addiction was all on me. It was fully my responsibility to show them that there was a man in me that not only loved them but also loved himself, enough to want more than just playing the blame game while clutching a bottle of liquor every day.

Please have faith that it's worth it. It's refreshing to think back on who I used to be compared to the man I am now. It's a great feeling of redemption after fighting for the best version of me to show myself and the people that matter to me. You too can enjoy that feeling once you start the change you need to make to control your behaviors and thoughts.

**Don't be the problem again!** After gaining control of my thoughts, and displaying better behaviors, there's another lesson I learned. Don't create unnecessary issues... By monitoring your thoughts and behaviors, you're preparing yourself to handle and address trouble, not start it. The more your mind is idle, not checking yourself, the easier it is for bad habits or distrustful behaviors like; lying, cheating, drug use, etc. can seem like manageable things. All you're doing is setting yourself up to fail. Again, and again! Don't make things harder for you than they must be. We all know life is crazy all on its own. Being in a pit of terrible choices is stressful. No one is putting a gun to your head causing you to do dumb stuff. It's all on you! If there is someone holding you at gun point to do things, then please seek help from the authorities! Sorry but in most cases, it's you that's causing the extra tension and getting off track due to the aimless reasons you give yourself to be lazy. That's one of the biggest factors of not staying in control. It's laziness. You start to feel the difference then suddenly start feeling the exhaustion of putting in more work. No need to keep going if you've slipped back into your old ways. Don't give up because you've stumbled a little. That's not the mindset we're trying to work on here. You indeed may find it easier to just give up being great or better. But why did you buy the book in the first place? Just to read something you already know or to get a different perspective on becoming the person you truly desire to be? I need you to believe that things will work out for you! The smarter you work the easier things will get and be! There's a wall that we all will face when making corrections to our lives. It's in you to break through that wall or get over it! That's when the fight to want better for yourself and others kicks in! It will help you push through to the greater side of your thoughts/mind.

**Affirm!** Look at the person in mirror and say, *"I'm better than I was yesterday, and I will be even better tomorrow! Today I will love myself so that I can love those who need me. I forgive myself for whatever I've done in the past. I forgive those that have wronged me. Today is the day I should focus on *insert whatever it is you need or want to accomplish*. No other day is more important than right now. I can do this!"* If it takes a week or a year, keep talking to yourself to correct yourself. The more you hear your own voice speaking positivity on your own life the more you'll believe it. Say it and it will manifest.

# Body/Health

**Health is wealth!** I remember hearing that for the first time thinking to myself what it meant. You don't think about it that deep until you're older. When you're young you think you'll live forever. This is true for too many men. There are quite a few guys I know now and knew growing up, including myself in my younger years, that wouldn't go to get a checkup. Others and I would only see a doctor if we were half dead. At least we may have thought we were dying. Are you that guy too? It is a damn shame we do ourselves that way as men. I believe it's the fear of the unknown that keeps us away. It should not be a second thought to do it. Imagine finding out you were at risk for serious illnesses ahead of time. Getting the right treatments or medications needed in time to avoid a life threating disease is lifesaving. You should have pride in knowing exactly what kind of condition you are in when it comes to your health. It eliminates most surprises. Going to the doctor's office because your wife, family or friend forced you to go, shouldn't be the only time you go. Why are you afraid? Hmm...? Because it was on you from day one to take care of yourself, but you were too stubborn to do so. Now you're regretting ever going once you find out you have a life altering condition. How will your kids look at that example you are setting? You think you're going to convince them to go get checked out regularly? You think any of your friends, or even your girlfriend or wife will listen to you about seeing about their health?

    You only have one body to focus on. None of us get to trade it in for a new one. Once we run it down in the ground because we didn't want to deal with doctors or "thought' we were fine while fighting with aches and pains daily, that's it. Maybe they're working on some form of tech modified arms, hearts, lungs, etc..., but I can only imagine what the price tag would be on a brand-new body! Why torture yourself with the discomfort of an aching lower back, a bad knee, tight muscles in your neck or a headache that keeps coming back days and days at a time? It is not worth it when all you had to do was get checked out. You don't have to go every day or every week. Not even every month, but please at least make it an annual thing to go to ensure you're okay. I would rather have a peace of mind with confirmation that I'm fine than living with uncertainty. You can't blame the doctors nor anyone else if you don't take care of yourself through the years if you find out terrible news. You can't do anything worth your wild without good health.

**Did you say food?** I was shocked when I found out that a lot of aches, pains and headaches come from what you put in your body. Yes, it's true! I can't say it enough how my entire body had shifted towards feeling better, more energized, less headaches and troubles when I switched up what I was eating. From heavy drinking, fried foods and sugary snacks every day for years, takes a huge toll on your overall health. Many may know this, but we don't link those things to the discomforts and body pains when they occur. We will make all kinds of excuses on how this and that could be from something else. We blame it on common issues like being tired from work or sleeping weird. We go as far as saying things like, "that always feels that way", not knowing that it resonates with the unhealthy eating habits we have.

    Some of it does have a bit to do with sleeping funny or not getting enough rest. I'm not a health expert or a sleep analyst but I'm telling you this from pure experience. I didn't know how seriously it effected my health, eating late at night then going right to sleep. Thinking it was the mattress or the amount of pillows I laid on that caused me to toss and turn all night. Even days I went to sleep at a good time but managed to creep through the night to the fridge to get a sweet snack. Again, going back to sleep to find myself nearly throwing up at times. Think about the times you've rolled over and over not knowing what it was keeping you up and uncomfortable. I know stress will do that but what you ate that day plays a major part too. You need to take your health just as serious as taking care of your finances. Imagine going after your dreams and goals but have to be in and out of the hospital because you didn't take care of yourself. In order to perform well, you must feel and be well. A daily workout, healthy food intake and hydration is essential for you. It's not to be ignored. The sooner the better. Don't ever think the time has to be right to take care of yourself. No one's going to do it for you. Well, hopefully no one has to no earlier than needed. Maybe in your later days, yeah but optimistically even then, you're still able to physically navigate through life on your on will and ability.

    The questions you must continue to ask yourself as you resume your terrible eating rollercoaster is, how am I going to achieve the goals or accomplish anything if my body doesn't allow me to? How am I going to do anything if I'm sick all the time due to unhealthy eating? Don't get me wrong, there are many conditions that we are born with, get passed down to us or that are out of our control. I get that. I'm talking about things you do have full management of. How your body is conditioned from an unhealthy lifestyle and neglecting yourself from the right foods and activities will cut everything short. Of course, we all want to live forever but that's not possible. It is possible to cut your life short. And it's possible living longer than you think because you cared and loved yourself enough to take care of you. It's impossible to live to your full potential if you do have good sustainable health. Please drink water too! It is crazy how many people hate drinking one of the most vital elements we have when it comes to helping our bodies. Water! Drinking water keeps you hydrated which improves the body in a big way. That alone is a great start as you focus on what foods are going to give your body the best results.

**Enhance what?** Do it as natural as possible. In the world we live in today, everything is changing rapidly. Including the food, from the fruits, vegetables, meats, etc.

that you're putting in your body. Warning! If you don't know by now... There are many enhancements being injected and processed in our food! They're spending big bucks trying to convince us that it'll make you stronger, faster, slim down and give you wings! Don't believe the hype! More than half of those "get healthy quick" products will not help at all. In some cases, they may make your overall health worse. One of the leading causes of unhealthy living and an early grave, is sugar! Sugar is your sweetest grim reaper. It's in nearly everything we eat. I advise you to start checking your packages, containers, etc. to see just how proud of sugar these companies are. Everything is loaded with sugar, which to most seems so innocent when you're a kid with a high metabolism. It's a slow yet deadly killer that has no mercy on the weak. I pride myself on refusing to continue down the sugar highway of death. Some of my family members today are battling diabetes. I didn't want to live like that the rest of my life. Taking medicines to offset something I can control on my own.

That's not a shot at them or anyone else, just the reality of what's at stake when you don't fight back before it's too late! If you can't pronounce the ingredients in what you're eating, then you probably shouldn't eat it! We go about our day mindlessly stuffing ourselves with some of the worst food on the planet. Especially here in America. Much of the food we eat here that has been approved by FDA, is banned in other countries. If you didn't know that already, sorry to burst your bubble. That's how bad some of our choices are. Again, I'm no medical expert but a lot of the sickness we have are from years of feeding ourselves some of the worst food in the world. Being less gassy feels good too! The trash I was putting in my body was giving me a ton of trapped gas, indigestion, and heartburn. I became familiar with what foods caused the most discomfort for me. Boy, were they all the tasty sweet and spicy stuff too. Please understand what foods trigger your body to react in a great way verses the foods that are basically breaking your body down.

**Try it, PLEASE!** Our bodies can only go for so long before breaking down from fueling ourselves with the wrong things. I just want to enlighten you if you haven't thought about this in depth. Please try eating whole foods. Try eating more fresh fruits and vegetables. I'm not telling you to go vegan or anything. Hate to sound like a dad. I'm no health nut. I love me some bacon. I don't eat nearly as much as I use to due to knowing how it impacts my health. I've heard about the many benefits there are to giving up meat. I'm personally not there yet. Starting my day off with fresh fruit has a totally different effect on my body's performance rather than eating four strips of bacon, egg and cheese sandwich with strawberry jelly. Man, that does sound good right now! No! Stay with me here! It will only satisfy your taste buds! Watch how your body functions after a week of better eating. Take notes on how you naturally have energy, less aches, pains while slimming down. Sounds like a winning plan to me. All from putting better choices of food on your plate.

I've done variations of fasting many times. Challenging myself to feel better and function organically from my body's own capabilities without any manufactured substances or products. There's no crash or after shock when your body responds to natural foods. Natural foods give you what all those other guys are saying you can get with enhancers! You will benefit from natural foods that help cleanse you to aiding you to become stronger. There's a natural remedy for just about everything health wise that you can imagine. With research, a huge decrease in my fast-food intake and more trips to the grocery store, I've managed to keep my weight down and have little to no headaches at all. For years I dealt with headaches without any clue of the cause. I no longer depend on over-the-counter drugs to soothe that discomfort. Other stiffness and soreness went away as well. That did more for me in other areas as a man and husband!

**Let's talk about Sex!** With great health comes great sex. That along should be enough of a reason to want your body to stay fit and all your limbs working properly. There are many foods and with exercising regularly can help improve your blood circulations in the right areas, improve your endurance to last longer and ultimately build your confidence. Drunk sex wasn't as good as I thought it was until I gave up alcohol and changed my health habits. That's right! I said it... The sex I'm having now is a hundred times better! Not only for me but for my wife as well. We both are reaping the benefits of what taking care of your health delivers. Since being the head of the house, when I made the change to do better about my body, it was easier for my wife to want to make sure she was taking care of herself too. Remember, it's contagious! When you have that love and support about something that's going to bring the best results to your health, it's priceless! That's what keeps me going as well. Someone to hold me accountable. When I want that triple cheeseburger and chili cheese fries for lunch or dinner, she's there to remind me that she will not allow it. It helps both ways. We continue to restrain each other when we're being weak to those bad food choices.

Even if you're not in a relationship or married, find a friend or family member that will speak up when they're around you to keep you honest. Let's go a little deeper when it comes to sex... *Pun not intended

# Sex

**Yes, Sex!** Like I said before, with good health, sex is amazing! But to most men, sex is great regardless! It's a gift and a curse. Sex is a gift from God as far as its purpose. To reproduce, create new life and for pleasure. Pleasures that can either be wonderful without any worries or an addiction that will tear your relationship, marriage and family apart. As a man committed to his wife, I've learned the hardest way possible the consequences of being unfaithful due to my addiction to sex.

One major thing I've learned was, **"Don't Follow the Flesh**!" It'll cost you more than you bargain for. A moment of pleasure can cause you a lifetime of regret and frustration. That's exactly what you get out of it, a moment. Usually less than ten minutes. Risking it all for ten minutes of pleasure. Don't kid yourself fellas. Sometimes less time than that. And who do you have to blame? That's right. Yourself! That's all it is when you're going about it the wrong way. If you have a wife or significant other, I advise you to work on that area. Be clear on what you expect in the bedroom. I'm serious!

Women put sex further down on the "List of Needs" than men do. In my opinion, men have a shorter list. Sex being within the top two to three things on our list! Top three easily for sure! If you're with someone that doesn't find sex being as important as it is to you, in the relationship or marriage, then you need to figure out how to adjust to that or kindly do you and them a favor. Let them go back into the pool of the single life! That will save them from you causing any pain and suffering because of your infidelity. You want to make sure that's not an area of temptation for you. It has and will always be a weakness for men. From my many years of many friendships, I'll say it is for sure for most of us, a challenging area...

**Sex on the mind...** One of the leading causes of divorces and break ups is lack of communication. But believe me, cheating is right there behind it, if not the number one reason. Men are always under attack! Women too but because sex is so high on our list of needs, it's going to be thrown at you one way or another. Which speaks volumes to why I talked about controlling what you put in your head. If you're walking around thinking you're the bedroom bully. If you think you can make any woman fall in love with you because of how good you put it down, then you're opening yourself up to be an easy target. Maybe you are the pied piper when it comes to a few you've been with or have a good sex streak of pleasing women, but I assure you, every woman's body and turn on is not the same. But you all know that already... If not... I'll get into that in just a second.

Just imagine your wife or girlfriend feeling that exact way. "Oh, I got that good stuff, I will have any man crazy about me if I give him some of my goodies." Any and every good-looking guy that speaks to her or inboxes her, you know what she's going to do. Just like you would... Right? She's going to respond because that's how she thinks. So, if that's your perspective whenever that attention comes your way from an attractive female, what do you think you're going to do? You won't stand a chance! Having some other woman flirting with you, stroking your ego, laughing at your corny jokes, ready and willingly, you're going to give it up within days, or weeks, maybe even right then and there! Could you live with your wife or girlfriend giving it up easily like that or at all because she thinks she's God's gift to "ALL" men (Which she is God's gift... But to "YOU"!)? Not for a split second would that be cool or acceptable. Funny how men feel that way. Not all men but quite a few.

**I am not a saint...** I'm guilty. I remember thinking I could get any woman I wanted while married to a gorgeous lady with a heart of gold! Because I was feeding myself that idea. Not that my wife wasn't satisfying me, I just told myself for so many years that sex was so important that if I weren't getting enough at home, someone else would give it to me. Only a fool thinks that way! A fool I was! Thinking it, turned into acting on it. When you're doing wrong, it follows you. You can't shake it until you truly turn away from it. Following the flesh almost cost me a ten-year marriage at the time, along with losing a beautiful family I created with an amazing woman! It's not worth it! I repeat... IT IS NOT WORTH IT! I'm just trying to get you to see it from a different angle. Like I said earlier, sex can be and is an addiction. Especially for the weak minded. Just like any other addiction, you will need help to curve those cravings. What better help to have than from your life partner, girlfriend, or wife.

**Sex Monster!** First step is admitting that you have a problem or is struggling with that area. Being aware that you have an issue or challenges is a reality check you must have within yourself. Once I was able to look myself in the mirror and say that I needed help, I was able to take a different approach. It's hard to admit that sex is a problem area for most men. We start as youngsters masturbating to sexy ladies on info-commercials and VS magazines.

Oh, just me? Riiiiight... We think nothing of it as we continue our sex adventure from teens into our adult hood. We never question ourselves on why some of us must have two, three or more women to satisfy our sexual needs. There is no one to blame but ourselves. We have created this uncontrollable appetite for sex. We find ways to ignore the root of the reasons why we cheat. How would any woman compete with a sex addiction she didn't help create?

**Her body is amazing, yet fragile!** How many times a week do you expect sex from your woman? I'm not judging, but if you think every day, then you clearly don't understand how the female body works. I can't speak for all the ladies. Through my experience and many talks, I've had with various women through the years, I have yet to meet a woman that truly can or is willing to have sex every single day. If you have, then you have met a unicorn! It is extremely rare! Women bodies are unique. If you think her body is going through some difficulties during that longer week of the month, wait until she gets pregnant. Again, I'm not the chairman for women's voices or their bodies. I didn't understand how crucial this was until we started having kids. Once I realized the amount of energy, work and rest women needed to birth a child and the aftermath, I started to see that wanting to just cum no matter what, was just a selfish ass way of thinking. That's why I've said it many times and still until this day that women are God's greatest creation. Never take it for granted to have a lady in your life that's giving you her temple for your pleasure and doing it to the best of her ability. Their bodies are constantly changing and adjusting. They do a damn good job making sure it's appealing to keep us wanting them through it all! That's a superpower too! A little gratitude does go a long way. You have to love her beyond her body. You have to find ways to make it more than just about sex. You have to penetrate more than just the physical parts of her.

**What's your credit score?** Everything you do other than just trying to poke her every day, helps you to get it when and how you want it. I call it building good "**Sex Credit.**" Since sex is high on the top of our list, right fellas? I make sure I build my sex credit with my wife. Sex credit is what you've done to ensure your wife, lady, girlfriend is in the mood to please you. Her mood determines the kind of sex you'll have as well. If you don't believe me then wait until you start screwing up and being lazy around the house. Watch how quick that sex credit goes tumbling down hill! Her mood will change and she's not going to do that thing you like! She may not do it for a while if you're not willing to build your sex credit score back up. *For more about it, check out one of my favorite books I wrote, "Sex Credit".

**Replace what with money?** Money is no match when you have a woman by your side rooting for you, pleasing you and loving you unconditionally because you are worth it. Not because you have a huge bank account. Giving her money is great. Not sure if any woman would disagree? I do know when you're helping with the major and small things around the house, with the kids, making her overall life easier, she will cherish that way more than any amount of money you can give her. Money does come and go. Trying to compensate her with money for your lack of participation as a dad or lover, money can't buy you that time back. Money also can't replace her needs for sex either. Remember that! She will indeed help you become a wealthy man. I'll talk more about that in the Financial/Investing part of the book.

**Who is she?** On the flip side we have to truly know our mate as well. What if she has had sexual trauma or experiences with sex, she never had the voice to speak on. Things that never crossed your mind because it's all about you and your sexual goals. This is something I personally highly recommend for men to do more of. Ask and get to know her past when it comes to sex. Not checking to see how many sex partners she has had, but understanding how she truly feels about it overall. Are there challenges mentally that causes her to not want to do certain things? Are there any insecurities or doubts within herself about her body that's causing her to hold back? Does she enjoy sex just as much as you do?

This is the approach you should have with your wife if you haven't had such a conversation or at least with the woman you plan on marrying if you haven't done so yet. This may not be the best idea if you just met her at the club, bar or grocery store yesterday. Understood? This is not for you to hold over her head either. I repeat! The information she shares, is to NEVER be thrown at her as an insult EVER! Do not guilt trip her by repeating it out of frustration because you're not getting what you want when it comes to the bedroom. You must do it with compassion and concern, not judging her. If that's something you can't stomach, then seek alternative ways to find out what she prefers and her comfort level in that area. It's worth it! She will want to mirror that effort you're putting in and the benefits of a woman feeling loved without criticism is priceless! Especially about sensitive information most women never get the opportunity to share with anyone, including their significant other.

**It's priceless!** So, imagine your lady being completely opened with you about herself. That's going to lead to a more fulfilling sex life. You have to be opened as well. Don't have her pour out her past or her feelings about sex and you stay closed in. Shutting her out of your past experiences won't help. She needs to know just as much about your desires and challenges too. Again, we want to make sure that sex is the least of our worries. I'm quite sure your wife, girlfriend, etc. wants to make sure they're doing and giving you all the right attention, you need in the bedroom. That will indeed reduce the amount pressure she feels when it comes to a sex appetite you have that she's unaware of. The more you all know about one another the easier it becomes for the both of you. She can be your lady in public and your nasty freak in the bed! Best of both worlds! A man's dream come true!

**Not this kind of self-love...** One last thing, that may help. I want to close this section talking about porn and masturbation. When it comes to pleasing yourself, that's part of what's causing some of the disconnect as well. It took me a minute to grasp how masturbating was affecting my sex life. Having the logic, that if my lady wasn't giving it up when I wanted and needed her to, it was way too easy for me to shrug my shoulders. I began to rely on the habit of watching porn. I would just go rub one out. I wasn't disciplined enough to wait until she was ready. Not being satisfied enough, I became a slave to only pleasing the sex monster in me. Inconsiderate to thinking if she just gave me a great night of sex, that she may need a night or two to recover. Again, I was being selfish and only thinking about me.

The more you keep your hands away from yourself and maintain your sex hunger, it'll help you perform better. It'll have you wanting her and her only. I gave up watching porn and masturbating because I only wanted to be pleased by my wife. I was able to have way more control of myself when she became the only trigger for me when it came to being sexually aroused. It showed in my affection towards her. Days she wanted to just cuddle was more acceptable. Days she would initiate sex more often than me, which was a very satisfying payoff for me. I wasn't just thinking about myself and pressuring her on the days she wasn't feeling her best. Cold showers do help too. For me they did...

**Take it one day at a time. You must want it for her and for yourself. Staying busy with a goal or two keeps you from being distracted too...**

**Let's talk about that now!**

## Mission/Goals/Dreams

**There's so much more out there!** When I think of a goal or dream, I think of a tailored direction. What direction are you going in? Are you spending your day to day, going about life with a clear map? I'm not saying you need to be freaking out right now if you're going about life that way. BUT! Let's change that as soon as possible. I felt lost for quite some time in my life. I didn't have anything to go after because I wasn't interested in anything. I didn't care about nice cars, designer clothes, gold rings, watches nor any kind of new sneaker fetish.

My only concern was the "right now" and what was happening in my life moment to moment. I was blindfolded by my unwillingness to pay attention to all the signs that were right before my eyes. Signs that were telling me that there was more in life I could do and discover. That way of thinking started when I was in grade school. It was passed down to me. I was not thinking outside the ridiculously small box I was conditioned to be in. Nor did I have any idea how to change that. Having parents (single mom, absent dad) that thought the same way their parents thought, didn't give me a fighting chance. Back then you were raised by two set of rules. Go to school, graduate, find a job then work there forever to survive. Or for some, let the government take care of you.

Don't do anything too crazy like dream of a life better than the one you have (living on welfare, section 8 and food stamps) or it will be taken away. I get chills just thinking about all the families and friends that settled for that government assistance way of living for far too many years! Again, I'm not saying this to shame anyone. I was raised in that kind of environment. I understand that people do need help. I get it… But…

**PLEASE do not limit yourself to that kind of thinking! It is poison!**


**Don't be afraid!** Is there anything that keeps you up at night? Something like a thought or a dream you can't stop having? Is there something that keeps flashing before your eyes, you can't seem to shake off? If you're experiencing these things, then that's a sign. We all have dreams but there are none like yours. I have yet to communicate with anyone else in my dreams while we both were sleep. Let me know when you do.

    Just like we all have our own dreams, we also have our own plans. Some may be similar but, in most cases, you have a gift that requires your attention. You have dreams that need your attention to fulfill them. The only way you're going to make your dreams come true is... Having a plan. That's a goal. A plan that circulates around those dreams you've had or goals you wrote down five years ago you never pursued. You need something to look forward to. That helps with keeping you focused. There's less idle time to be distracted by other women or keeping you in circles of people you don't belong in. You must have something you're chasing. Not women! Unless it's the one woman you've been pursuing that's going to add that missing piece to your happiness and peace.

Remember from the previous chapter how that will turn out. A plan makes it real by removing it from your mind on to paper. Taking that dream you continue to have and dissecting it. Breaking it down to understand it so you can go after it.

First step after writing down your dreams, ideas, and goals, is believing you can achieve them. Please, have faith that it can happen for you! Too often we shy away from those ideas because we feel we're not worthy. Look at it like this, imagine that Kobe Bryant, Martin Luther King Jr., Chadwick Boseman, Steve Jobs or Michael Jackson didn't believe what they accomplished couldn't be done by them? They would have deprived us of their awesome and amazing abilities and world changing victories!

They all had faith in themselves and their dreams. Please believe that something positive you desire can be possible. Something that's going to bring not only yourself joy but as well as something that will be benefiting all your loved ones. There isn't anything too wild that can't be done. Especially if you plan it out, then execute the steps to move closer to the finish line.

**Don't wait on the applauds!** One thing about your dreams and plans... Many people won't be excited about them like you are. There's going to be some of the closest people to you that won't support you. That's fine! Don't hold that against them. Especially the ones that have that poor man's mentality. Use that to your advantage. Prove it to yourself how much it means to you to achieve those goals. Again, they're YOUR plans and dreams!

You must put in the work regardless of who is not helping or rooting for you. No one can discourage you from going after the things that's meant to be for you. Not even you! Again, don't take it too personal when that negative response comes from those you expected to help you. It's going to happen. That should only be fuel to your fire to accomplishing all your goals and plans. Don't make anyone feel bad about it either. You're not entitled to receive anyone's blessings about anything you're doing. Allow it to come organically. Let them have their doubts. But not once, do you engage with guilt tripping anyone.

For me, it was writing. I used to write poems, rhymes/lyrics and short love quotes. I started on a book many years ago but never finished it. Writing was something I could do but didn't have the patience or dedication to do it. I bragged about it back then thinking I was doing something everyone would praise me for. It lasted a few months until I didn't get the feedback I had hoped for. I didn't let anyone down but myself. It never left my dreams. For years I kept seeing these books and stories flashing in my thoughts. Dreams of me writing novels. I had to find the courage to do it for myself. I had already made myself look bad for announcing something I wasn't putting in the work to accomplish. I was quiet about it for the most part until I was finished with my first fiction book, "Which Way to Go"! Now I can't stop writing because I genuinely believe in me.

The support I didn't have when I first released my first book has changed. The doubters are supporting me as well as the naysayers. It was a "Win Win" for me! I had a dream and I put it on paper, literally. Since I started my writing journey, allowing my dreams to come true, it has kept me busy. It keeps me paying attention to the things that matter the most. It makes my wife and kids proud. The key was the habits and the personal system I discovered that worked for me.

**What are you waiting for?** If I can do it, so can you. If you haven't started yet, do it now! No one has the map to the fountain of youth. I highly doubt that there is one. None of us are getting any younger. The quicker you can start planning to achieve your dreams and goals, the quicker your life will change and lead you in a positive direction. You will have your own plans and something only you can focus on. You won't have time watching everyone else live their dreams, you will be too busy making yours come true. Own your days and make time for what you desire. Your plans can lead to financial freedom. Freedom to do what you enjoy the most. Living out your dream with the people you love the most. Imagine that. Living a life with the power to be fully committed to your goals and ideas. That's priceless. That's a life worth living for sure! Let's jump into that...

Financial freedom...


Let's talk money!

# Finances/Money

**Dollar Dollar Bills!** Ever heard of the saying, "Money can't buy you happiness..."? But, if you're like everyone else I know, you want to find out for yourself! Money will not buy happiness. However, it will make some things easier for you! It is very necessary to have financial stability in this world. As a man, father, and husband, it's a great feeling being a provider. It is nice being able to go out to buy whatever it is you need. I say "NEED" because too many people are broke due to only spending their money on whatever they "WANT" while failing to secure their needs. Unless you're a farmer, harvesting crops and raising livestock then you're going to need money to feed your family. Are you a carpenter, electrician, plumper, roofer all in one? Again, you will need money to provide a home for your family.

Growing up in the environment I was in, money was never a part of any conversation.

You know things were hard based on the conditions of the house you lived in, the hand me down clothes you wore, what was on your plate at dinner and if the lights were turned off every other month. That is a tough life to live for anyone. Who do you blame for that? I never blamed my mom for the way I was raised when it came to understanding how money works. I would have to go deeper than just her. Like, I said, they inherited that way of thinking. Today, I would have to point at the man in the mirror.

Knowing what I know now, I would be a fool to sit back and not choose a better way of living financially. I didn't get any lessons in school about it. I didn't have many friends raving about it. None of that. It was the tough lessons I learned when it came to money. Can you believe that? It's not even taught in school. With the number of resources, we have now like the internet, there are countless ways to be educated on how money can make your life easier. Don't be afraid of that conversation. Now or never! Now is the time to get control of your money. Especially if you have a family that depends on you.

**Fake money?** For too long people have always tried to appear as if they're more well off than they really are. Let me say this as well. Fellas be careful starting a relationship based off buying that young lady all the best and fanciest stuff to woo her over. It's risky because you're going to have to keep that spending up. You can't blame her if you're trying to buy her attention. You started it and more than likely, some women will expect that the entire relationship. You're telling her it's okay to have whatever she wants whenever she wants it regardless of how much it is. Even if it's going to cost you everything to do it. She'll be happy but you'll be stuck deciding if you're going to eat or she's going to get those new heels. I do agree that women deserve nice things but, there are ways you can do it without going broke.

People love to look like they have money. It's a never-ending trend unfortunately. The majority of poor people like to show off to impress the people around them. They go out and buy all the things they can't afford. The entire time they're behind on their rent/mortgage, light bill and one note away from getting their car towed. They have all the nice clothes and shoes, eat out at fancy restaurants daily. Doing it all as they share those highlights on social media or talk about it amongst friends, yet they have nothing put aside for a rainy day. What's the point of doing all of that? Why try to impress people that don't give a damn about you?

The same people they're trying to show off in front of are the same people that won't help them pay a dime towards any of their bills if they ever need assistance. Why should anyone help you if you appear or campaign your life as if you're a baller and money isn't a thing? Do not be these people! If you spend all your money on the latest designer shoes and clothes but don't have your bills caught up, emergency money on the side, life insurance or any assets to leave your family when you check out, then your priorities aren't lined up right.

You're not being smart with your money! If you'll spend money on fast food or choose to go to an expensive place to eat instead of choosing to get more food for your money by going to the grocery store, again, your money is not going to weigh out in the long run. Especially if your fridge is empty and you have to wait days before more money comes in! NOTHING is wrong with buying fast food or grabbing a nice shirt or belt for yourself, mainly if you've worked your ass off for it. I'm saying this for those that choose that first. Those that spend first then try to figure out how they're going to pay their bills or how to invest their money last.

**Pay Attention to Real Money!** How many CEOs, business owners you know or seen in public or on TV that look like they have money? Not a lot from what I've seen over the years. They're spending habits are much different. I say that because that's what I started to pay more attention to. I had to change the way I thought about money. I looked at money as a tool to get more stuff, to satisfy my wants. Which is why I stayed broke! When I started comprehending how the rich stayed rich, it was a clear picture and I needed to adjust accordingly. It was the creating money part that blew my mind the most. Instead of finding more ways to spend money, the rich find more ways to create money. If all you've done was spend your whole life, then yes, it's a brutal habit to break. If you've reached that boiling point of "being sick and tired of being sick and tired" when it comes to being broke, then you know for a fact it's not a pleasant life to live at all.

One way that made it simple for me to transition from spending carelessly all the time to knowing where my money was going, I asked for help from someone I trusted. Like I said earlier, your wife or girlfriend can help make you a wealthy man! It was having a woman on my side that wanted more out of life then living check to check or trying to live a lifestyle that cost way more than what we could keep up with. My wife wanted to have money and a steady flow of it just as much as I did. We both started to hate spending money we knew we didn't have on things we really didn't need. When you have someone that wants a certain income, it helps when it comes to learning how money can work for you! It helps when you have someone holding you accountable when you're about to give your money away. Cause again, money is a touchy subject.

**Money Talk...** When was the last time you sat down with your wife or significant other to have an in dept discussion about your finances? Have you ever? Do you just hope for the best and handle your part of the bills while keeping a few dollars in your pocket for yourself? One thing I hated when I was an acholic was thinking we had more money in our account than we did. Yes, I said OUR account. I never understood why so many married couples kept personal bank accounts. If that's working, more power to you. I'm never going to slander anything that is working. I've seen more arguments and distrust in marriages due to the husband and wife believing that they had their own money when it came to paying for things. In some cases, they rarely disclosed the amounts they had stashed away. Which goes back to the lack of communication I mentioned when it comes to one of the leading causes of divorce and break ups. If you're in a relationship, then yes, it is perfectly fine to have separate accounts. Talk about hoping for the best... If you're practicing joint bank accounts before tying the knot, then you are one brave soul! Or that's some serious sex she's giving up. Just kidding about the sex part. I don't recommend doing it before marriage because it's way easier to break up than to get a divorce. That's an ex you'll hate forever if she runs off with all your money! The one that got away... Hope that helps!

    My thoughts were, why would we have separate accounts if we're in this together until death do us part. That includes all of us. Our minds, bodies and ALL our money, right? As if they have an exit plan waiting to execute at any time things go south. Again, I'm not judging you or your marriage if this is what works best for you. I tried it and it sucked for me personally. I didn't like having to remember to pay for anything when bills were due or create a budget. We both work, our checks deposits in an account together then my wife handles all the bill payments. I wasn't helping if I was swiping the card all the time without making her aware of when and what I was spending money on. It takes work! And a lot of trust but it's worth it.

    Once we had the same way of thinking about money, we decided to do what the rich do. **Create more money...** Find a system that works. A system that will generate results. Money is the result! Working a nine to five is one for sure way to bring in income to help support your family and habits. But what if you had a system of creating income that eventually worked on its own? What if you had a money tree? No, not in your backyard you could go pick one hundred dollars bills from. Having a goal is one thing, that's direction. However, when you achieve that goal, what usually happens? In many cases, you result back to your same old ways or you give up taking it to the next level. Having a system creates that never ending cash flow. Endless goals and endless income. That system is a lifestyle. Having a money tree is having an invention, real estate, optional trading, published books or music, etc. that will give you the financial freedom you desire. When you have behaviors in line with the focus you need then you will dedicate your time and energy up front to secure your money trees. It's working on your own ideas and plans that will eventually pay off later.

The world we live in now isn't like it used to be. Working for a company for 30 years, with a 401k and pension was the best thing since sliced bread, back then! Most companies have eliminated their pension plans, more are shutting down and the 401k isn't worth much with the roller coaster market we have. Let's not talk about the endless fees and taxes you will have to pay! More people are having to work two or more jobs to make ends meet.

Instead of being employed by someone else for the rest of your life, focus on hiring yourself. Work your job, then make time to work on your money tree. If you're giving the corporate world eight to nine hours of your life five days a week, then please give yourself at least half of that time to work on your plans. Get a side hustle that can potentially turn into your own business. Start writing that book, movie or tv show idea, then publish it or pitch it. Start recording your music. Spend time working on that computer program or that social media app you believe in. It becomes a lifestyle when you start to do it automatically. YOUR money trees are planted and getting the right attention to grow every day when you're working on your ideas. Every minute and hour you put in; you're stepping closer to that financial freedom you dreamt of. One day at a time.

**Why do it?** Do it because of your "Why"! My "Why" was breaking the money curse my family was under. The reason I wanted to do it was because I want my children's children and so on to have a fighting chance to make it in this world without having to struggle like I did when it comes to money. My "Why" is my wife and kids... My mom and sisters and a few friends that are rooting for me. You too are a part of my "WHY"! I want you to become a better man, father and husband! So, what is your "WHY"? Your "Why" will lead you. Your "Why" must be bigger than you. So big that you leave footprints.

## Legacy/Footprints

**Because of others...** Everything you put in; you should have something to show for it. Not in just a physical form but knowledge as well. Leaving a blueprint based on what you've witnessed and experienced to give to the generation after you is impactful. Your kids should have footprints to follow to achieve greater things than you. You should be able to equip them with methods and understanding on how to maneuver through life's obstacles with less roadblocks. You must have things lined up to give those coming behind you a fighting chance to make it. Do it for them! They are counting on you, more than it may seem.

Imagine how easier your life would have been had your father or grandfather left you with a business, property and money to get your life started. What if they educated you on how to start a business, financial literacy and you saw through their actions how to do it from the ground up. If you had that, you are truly beyond blessed. That's even more than enough of a reason for you to carry the torch making sure that doesn't end with you. If you're like me, which is most of us, then you've had to work hard for everything you have. That doesn't excuse you from fighting for better for the next generation. You owe it to them!

There should be a sense of pride when it comes to knowing your hard work won't go in vain. If you've reached a point of hopelessness as if you've blown that opportunity already, then you obviously hadn't been paying attention to anything in this book. At any given moment or second of your life, you can change for the best. If you've worked on all the areas, I've mentioned in this book then I know for sure you are heading towards a legacy worth leaving footprints for. Again, you have developed positive habits which leads to greatness! Greatness is defined by your own standards. I hope that after reading this book that you will elevate your standards to a level you truly desire to achieve. Some people are satisfied with the bare minimum. Ask yourself this... Are your standards set high enough to create generational wealth? Are you just managing your own needs and wants while you're here? Who will benefit from the lifestyle you're living right now? Will your children or grandchildren reap anything from what you're sowing?

Those are the questions I had to ask myself. I didn't like the answers at the time I first thought about them. It was enough to make me change the direction. It forced me to get creative and set forth a solid plan. It inspired me to write this book. I needed something to remind me that it's not just all about me. It's about those that look up to us and depend on us. It's about your life, your wife, significant other, your kids and their kids. I encourage you to think deep about those questions and your answers. It matters!

*You are needed. You are loved. You make a difference. From being there for your kids, to being honest about your mental health with your significant other. You are appreciated even when no one tells you. You are the head. You can be better. You can become the man, father and husband you need to be. I love you and believe in you. Make it happen! Thank yourself later...*

www.ingramcontent.com/pod-product-compliance
Lightning Source LLC
Chambersburg PA
CBHW070404240426
43661CB00056B/2533